Breaking Point

Chalay Hedge

Breaking Point

Breaking Point
Copyright © 2015 by Chalay Hedge

All rights reserved. No part of this book may be reproduced or transmitted in any form or by any means without written permission from the author.

ISBN- 13:978-0996124942

Edited by Ashley Rhame

Publisher:
Rare Press
Roanoke, VA

Printed in USA

Rare Press Publishing

Collection of Poetry

Dedication

There is one person that will forever and always have a special place in my heart. Anyone who knows me understands who I mean. I lost this person by doing everything I could to push him away. If there is anything I can tell you about love; it's never turn away no matter how scared you are. Embrace it, because just as it was given, it can be taken away. I love you, David. Forever, like I promised.

To my fair and beautiful sister, Love Roslyn Graham you were gone all too soon. Though we all wish a million times over that we could take your place, we knew you to be strong and overcame as much as you could. And now your pain is over.

We love you LoveBug! Fly high baby girl ❤

Introduction

Hello, my beautifully blended fans of reasonable and outlandish literary diamonds in the rough. As far as what possessed you to buy this book, I can't say, but for the act itself, I can only tell you that my heart was poured into these pages. You are holding in your hands a piece of my life, pleasure, excitement, pain, sadness, need, and self-loathing. All necessary and expected parts of human life, but some people in this world are better at writing their feelings than expressing them out loud; I, unfortunately, am one of those people. But it makes for powerful words and an eccentric read for an onlooker such as your self. So please, enjoy this piece of me that I am giving you. It's on the house.

Open your eyes,
Open your heart,
So that humble love,
Can play its part,
Breathe through your ears,
And hear through your nose,
You've got to get strange,
And see where it goes,
Run through the halls,
Of a dead silent school,
Tear down the posters,
And dive in the pool,
There's only one life,
And to live it my dear,
You have to get strange,
You have to get weird.
Life is an experience.

Surprise Ending

Who knew?
Who knew I'd become broken?
Who knew I'd be damaged?
Who knew I'd become lost?
When love just seemed to vanish.
Who knew I'd become heartless?
Who knew I'd become angry?
Who knew that he was capable,
of putting them before me?
Who knew all the secrets?
Who knew all the lies?
Who knew what he told me,
As he gazed into my eyes?
Who knew he would break me?
Who knew I would crumble?
Who knew I'd be fighting,
Instead of being humble?
Who knew I would doubt him?
Who knew I would question?
Who knew that our love,
Was nothing but a lesson?
Who knew he would end it?
Who knew he'd get tired?
Who knew he'd take my heart,
And throw it in the fire?
Who knew it was over?
Who knew it could be?

Who knew our love would end,
By a person I thought was sweet.

Teenage Love Affair

He winked at her,
She noticed him,
He complimented her,
She smiled at him,
He called her beautiful,
She felt her heart warming,
He was heartbroken,
She comforted him,
He wanted her,
She wanted him,
He kissed her,
He said he loved her,
And she started to fall,
He told her he needed her,
She started to believe him,
He made things sound so sweet,
She gave him everything she had,
But suddenly, he was gone,
His feelings reduced to calm apathy,
But she still noticed him,
She still smiled at him,
Her heart was still warm for him,
She still comforted him,
She still wanted him,
And he still had everything she was,
And she thought she deserved him,
Even if he didn't deserve her.

III.

(Girl sits hunched over, cross-legged in a empty, dark room. A loaded shotgun sits at her feet, beside a bottle of Paul Mason. Her hair falls around her face, shielding it. She raises her head slowly.)

I'm dead.
I must be dead.
I'm supposed to be dead…
I must be a freaking superhero.
Because I've had my heart ripped out, shredded, and stuffed back into the malicious hole from whence it came…
Love? (Scoffs)
THAT'S A JOKE.
You think you love somebody, you think you'd give your all to them and then they…
Never mind.
It's not like you really care anyway.
No one cares…
No one wants TO CARE, that's the problem.
And the few that do end up like me.
'Cause I used to care…
I used to starve myself so he could eat!
And look at me now.
Still starving.
But instead I'm starving for something else.
Attention, maybe?
Or maybe it's something else…
I want a boy with his shirt unbuttoned, walking beside me on the beach after dark.
I want antidepressants that don't make me tired.
I want to make love to my husband on our wedding night at a beach while the waves lick at our toes…

I want children.
A boy and a girl,
With hope in their eyes and innocence in their hearts,
That look up from coloring to say,
"I love you, mommy."
Yea….
(Laughs bitterly, clicking of metal)
Whatever.
I hate that I want so desperately things
That are so unobtainable.
I hate that I'm wallowing in my pity.
I hate the person I've become…
I hate the person you made me!
You don't even care, but I knew that.
Maybe I'll be someone different the next time around.
(BOOM.)

Ballad For A Nerd

My love talks nerdy to me,
He says he's my Gagar,
And when I don't get it,
He tells me it's the love fox from Pokémon,
I never watched that show,
But,
I liked the way he smiled when he said it.
My baby speaks Spanish to me,
He says things like,
"Esa sonrisa es Hermosa,"
And,
"Te amo mas de las estrellas y mas de las olas en el mar,"
And even though I'm fluent in the language,
I'd rather hear him speak it than anyone else.
My angel whispers poems to me,
His words are so simple,
But they're always sugary sweet,
Like,
"You're the flour to my tortilla, lady,"
I just kiss him and say,
"Tell me another."
I know I tell him I'm not good with words,
But, truthfully,
I just can't compete with,
Him.

True, Unmeasured, And Malicious

You can only say you've felt true pain when,
You sacrifice your beauty and health,
You hide your tears to spare their feelings,
You smile even though you're hurting,
All to make them happy,
Until its 3 in the morning and you're standing on a rooftop,
With your feet on the edge, vertigo sweeping over you,
And all you can think of is how jumping off would end the pain,
For you and for them,
Until your body is 20 pounds lighter from all the tears you've cried,
All the restless nights and the meals you've missed,
The sleepless nights, the worrying, the stressing,
Until you can't stand to look at that being in the mirror,
Because you hate everything you see,
Until your tears are reduced to blood,
And arguments are reduced to thin slits,
That pour over your arms, legs, and thighs,
As you weep silently on the floor of the shower,
You haven't felt true pain,
Until the one you love,
The one you'd die for,
Throws all of that away
Like it didn't ever mean anything in the first place.

Psalm

Metaphorically,
I would be called a shell of my former self,
A ghost of who I once was,
And though I tried to hide it,
Instead you came and fixed me,
With crimson wrists and teary eyes,
I was plucked from the crowd and smiled upon,
You placed me in your beauty chair,
Beginning the long and arduous process,
With your expertly skilled fingers,
You took your shears and snipped away,
At the sadness,
The hurt,
The pain,
The depression,
And framed my shining face with it,
Upon seeing the hurt and sickness
Weighing down my eyes,
You frowned and brightened my eyes with your smile,
Until my eyes shone like gold,
You rose,
With me in the palm of your hand,
And the world saw me,
And for the first time since I could remember,
I smiled,
And you smiled back at me,
As the people began to stare,

I began to shrink away,
But you caused me to stiffen my back
And look upon our people with confidence,
And you told me that I was a beautiful piece of artwork,
And I believed what see you as truth,
You built me,
You repaired me,
You saved me,
And I am eternally grateful to you,
My savior,

Selah.

I Promise, I'm Over It

I would ask for you to come lay with me,
But what would that really accomplish?
I'd beg you softly to stay with me,
But I still hear your broken promise,
Forever seemed to come and go,
Our happiness a passing phase,
Like summertime to falling snow,
The infatuation just went away,
Our perfect high school romance,
Now reduced to heartache and pain,
Back then we used to laugh and dance,
And take love's humble name in vain,
Barefoot atop the burning coals,
We weathered every storm,
Resilient as the springtime foals,
And fresh as summer corn,
Though our love has come and gone,
I've cherished all I could,
You speak of things like moving on,
You know it hurts but it's for good,
"Life's too short," I heard you say,
And bitterly I laughed,
Cause he was all I had today,
And tomorrow he'll be my past.

Phases

With beautiful, elegant posture,
She graces the room with her presence,
He voice as soft as satin and her hair flowing like a river,
Her long, graceful legs lead her to her seat,
And even the chair seems to bow to her,
Thankful to hold her,
She smiles, and the room glows,
And as her hand waves,
The wind stops so that she can wave freely,
The people offer her gold and the finest silk,
And gracefully she accepts the gifts of her subjects,
Not unlike a queen,
Her pearl pink lips form effortlessly around her words,
And the people gawk and stare,
For she is a goddess among peasants,
But,
As the masses recede,
And the years pass,
Her fame falls by the wayside,
And she sits,
Alone in her ivory tower,
Holding a mirror up to herself,
Disgusted by what she sees,
And she realizes she is cold hearted and evil,
And her beauty is worth less than a penny,
And she is in her old years and dying swiftly,
Because she is in fact, Alone.

Shattered.

Tonight,
His eyes will grace the slender frame of a tiny girl from a foreign country, whose throat is raspy from screaming the angry words to her favorite song. His hands will dance along her body as he slips it under her shirt and brushes a spot he shouldn't have touched and he'll mumble that it was an accident; his nose will greet the seductive scent of Victoria's Secret, and his lips will pucker as she leans in close for a kiss, and they'll kiss like they've been married for years. As they sit under the telltale moon, drenched in the light as the clouds move swiftly across the sky, moved by the newness of their juvenile love. He'll get tangerine colored lipstick all over his lips, his cheek, his shirt, and go home reeking of Pure Seduction, and he'll crawl into bed promptly after slipping off his party clothes (but never his socks) at five in the morning, and just before he falls into sleep fit for a king, he'll have a passing thought of someone he forgot about, something he forgot to do…

Far away,
She'll realize she hasn't heard from him all day, and as her phone lights up with a message, she'll collapse into tears, wondering what she did that was so wrong to make him want to kiss another girl, the exact same way he kissed her…

Dreams, Unhinged

That couple never gets married,
You never live happily ever after,
Your first crush isn't your last,
Your first heartbreak isn't either,
You never get your white picket fence,
Or a big house and 2.5 kids,
You don't meet your soul mate in high school,
And your friends don't love you like they say they do.

It's taken me 17 years to figure out
That the entire life I knew was a lie,
Take it from me kid,
You and God are all you got.

New

As the last few moments of
Gracious darkness dwindled in the earth,
Everything seemed so still and quiet,
Like the last few moments of sleep before waking up,
And as the sun broke zealously over the clouds,
The earth did arise,
As if someone had turned up the dimmer on the lights,
The sky became an explosion of pinks, oranges,
Lavenders, and maroons,
The clouds bowed in introduction of father sun,
The moon watched from afar as her lover
Lit up the world with his vivid smile
Before slowly sinking behind the clouds
Without so much as a whisper,
Everything brightened,
The very presence of the sun gave things life,
The moon was eerie and beautiful,
But the suns beauty was abundantly birthing,
And even nature seemed to be
Irrevocably in love with his candid adagio,
As the trees erected and the water began to flow,
The sun began to laugh,
And in doing so his light spread over the land,
So I watched nature awaken,
And I felt their secrets,
At five in the morning,
Sitting on a tin roof, in North Carolina

Spoken By A True Poet

They say Elijah Muhammad was a prophet,
But men say so many things
There's not much to believe,
They say the road to heaven is going through hell,
Well I've been through hell so, honey,
Ain't no going back for me.
Men lie and women lie but one things is true,
No matter what they say,
Love looks like you.
She smells like you, she walks like you, even a similar smile.
Love doesn't lie, no matter what is said, no matter what design.
Love isn't lust, although the feels the same.
Love has its own feel, own thoughts, it's own name.
Love isn't sex, though to some it feels the same,
Love isn't hurt, although that's what some may claim.
Love is...
And exists between two...
Two souls, two hearts, two people that grew,
Into one love, so let them say what they must.
Love is too strong to be stifled by lust,
Too real to be captured in sex,
Too powerful to be stopped by an ex,
Love is pain and a beautiful struggle.
Love never dies; it lives on and doubles,
It triples repeatedly,
love settles the score.
So if you say you love me,

Then say no more.
-Marcus Bingham

Don't Get Me Wrong

I'm not bitter,
Just broken,
I've had a shaky past,
My heart's tender,
No poking,
And stay off the grass,
Why bother?
You always end up hurting,
You ask, I titter,
I've spoken,
You can kiss my…
Class is where I saw you,
And how I wish I could forget,
But your smile was so slick,
Like the ball through the net,
Even now I can't shake,
The feeling I used to have,
While you would smile in my face,
Then walk that girl to class,
Should I have been wary?
Should I have just listened?
I guess it's too late,
I should have paid attention,
The signs, the signs,
Though they were everywhere,
I was blinded by my heart,
(Sigh) I really cared.

Was all our struggling for naught?
Man, you're all I've got…

Daddy's Little Princess

I remember the pig I made for you,
That you hung up on the wall,
And no matter how many years passed,
You would never take it off,
I remember when I used to get fevers,
And you had to miss work to be with me,
But you would never complain or gripe,
We'd go through our days peacefully,
I remember when I got older,
I started to think you were unfair,
Because my brother got to do things,
And you saw but didn't care,
I remember when our family split up,
And you moved away from me,
And though you were 2 hours away,
You drove me to school every day, faithfully,
I remember when I moved in,
And for a while it was just you and I.
Then your wife and her kids came,
And I had to let some things slide,
It took me a while to get settled,
And sometimes I'd still rather it be us
But I'm growing into a woman now,
So I have to grow up and adjust,
You're all I have, Dad,
When people have come and gone,
And I don't want that lady to come in,

And wreck our weakening bond,
I'm not a jealous kid, I swear,
But sometimes you just miss your dad,
The way he was before his wife,
Because he wasn't all that bad,
Sure, we've had our ups and downs,
But no family comes out perfect,
I miss the way we were before,
Because those days were worth it,
Daddy, we miss you, come back home,
Your family needs you back,
Work can wait a day or two,
But we can't, I promise that.

A Poem For Love

Baby girl,
You're beautiful,
You don't have long hair,
Or light skin,
Or whatever else society deems perfect,
But you are.
From your head to your tiny little toes,
You are wonderfully splendid,
You are beautifully irritating,
And you are the best little baby anyone could hope to meet,
I'm glad I could spend time with you in my arms,
And I'm glad I called you my neighbor,
My little sister,
My friend,
You will never find spunk like you've got, girl,
You'll never find that thing,
'Cause you've got something,
Little Love,
You've got it,
I'm sorry I didn't watch you more,
I'm sorry I didn't come back like I said I was,
I promised you,
But now I'm gone,
But I'll see you again,
Soon, as soon as I can,
I've watched you go from a little chunky baby,
To a slender and sleek toddler,

And I love every inch and curve of you,
You're perfect girl,
Don't let anyone tell you different.
Remember that Bratz doll I gave you?
I know you lost it,
But that was my favorite doll,
That's why I kept it,
But I gave it to you,
And for a while you had a piece of me,
When the cancer began to take your little, beautiful body,
I watched you get smaller and smaller,
But Little Love was a fighter,
You didn't give up, baby,
You kept kicking and swinging,
And I watched your hair get long,
I watched your legs get chunkier,
And I watched you get stronger,
I want you to know that you were always perfect to me,
And even though I rolled my eyes sometimes
Like when you would walk up to the door and knock and say,
"Hey, Neighbor!" And keep saying it until we answered,
I loved every minute I got to spend with you,
Little Love, I t breaks my heart that I didn't come back when I said I would,
It was my intention to see you,
Before you got so sick,
And I'm here too late,
But I still want you to know,
That you're an angel,

And you're the most perfect little baby I've ever met.
I love you LoveBug.

Queen

Her heart is broken,
Her hands are bloody,
They're ragged from the fight,
Her lips are swollen,
Her knees are weak,
But her eyes are black as night,
Her voice is shaking,
Her feet are dragging,
There's vomit on her sweater,
Her tears are streaming,
Body bleeding,
But she still looks better than ever,
She stands up tall,
Her head held high,
Never missing a beat,
And though its hard,
She stands and fights,
Until she achieves her feat,
This is the girl you need to marry,
This is the girl you need,
A girl who knows how to fight,
And more importantly,
How to bleed.

We Were Screaming Silently

Not many have the chance to see me,
Unhinged like that,
But you did.
You saw me facing all of my problems,
Realizing my biggest dreams,
Screaming in an empty room
Which no longer belonged to me.
Your voice trembled over your lips,
Watching this monster I had become,
The arguments had gotten more frequent,
The breakups became longer and longer.
And we were screaming,
You and I screamed for each other,
My soul pounded the insides of my body,
Waiting for someone,
Anyone,
You,
To help me.
You were a coward,
And I was just a lonely girl,
Sweeping the floor of an almost empty house
While listening to terrifyingly haunting music,
But this is not a love poem,
In fact I think it might be quite the opposite,
This is about falling out of love,
Realizing that you're lonely
Even in the midst of the person you love the most,

That's pain,
And you watched as the person you claimed to love
Shoved herself off of the deep end,
Too scared and too weak to plunge in after her,
I'll never forgive you for that,
Along with other things like stolen kisses
Between you and girls that claimed to be my friends,
Along with the words said in my absence
Those made everyone hate me,
And I'd never know why they hated me,
But you kept that a secret.
You will never gain my respect,
You will never again have my love,
Do you remember that day?
The day I shed so many tears over you
We sat in the grass talking about life,
And you were late because well…
Because you always are,
That was the day we fell out of love
And into existence,
But neither one of us had enough courage
To tell the other person otherwise,
I didn't because I thought I needed you so much,
And you didn't because you had never known that type of love,
I understand,
But sometimes,
When I think about you,
I can still hear it,
I scream, silently,

My heart screams,
And I wonder if you do too.

New Leaf

I could never let you scar me,
I could never let you win,
I could never let you ruin my soul,
And my happiness within,
I couldn't make you love me,
But I can find someone that will,
That treats me like the Queen I am,
Until I've had my fill,
You could never take me back there,
No matter how you tried,
I walked too far along this path,
Still drenched in tears I've cried,
I could never let you scare me,
Being the woman I've become,
I'm smarter now and wiser,
YOU are the war I've won,
I smile like a belt of stars now,
And laugh like almond milk,
Smooth and rich my joy pours out,
My skin as soft as silk,
My hair drops like a waterfall,
My beauty all so fresh,
Things you never got to see,
Before you up and left,
I could never lose this person,
This woman I've become,
Because as I sit and think my dear,

You're my favorite war I've won.

Love Is

It's like a breath of fresh air,
After a long and strenuous night,
All alone,
Smothered in the darkness and agony,
Straining and groaning from lack of oxygen,
Locked in an airtight casket,
I thought I knew what this was,
But really I had no idea,
My mind was cloudy with childhood love and lust,
And what I thought I knew,
I didn't,
I can say I've felt it,
The way love grabs you up and makes you feel as if that can be all you know,
Until you're alone,
At 3:22 in the morning,
Dangling out a window,
Crying all the tears you couldn't before,
It changes you,
Love does,
And more than anything you want to scream,
Not for joy or out of agony,
But to see if you still can,
After all your dreams and desires have subsided,
And you let someone come in and be your heart,
You can still find it in you
To be the person you once were,

But to anyone that's ever been in love,
Real love,
It isn't possible to be the old you again,
It takes too much of the old you away,
Until you're forced to produce a very much
Diluted version of yourself,
And start from scratch,
Because they killed the person you once were,
Now, more than anything,
I desire laugh at a stupid movie on a Wednesday night
And drink strawberry soda,
I desire to scream like Indians in the falling rain
And dance with the cool, sporadic drops,
I want to go back as if I can start all over,
I want to love someone like I'll never grow old.
I want life again,
I want to share a life with nature and the heavens above,
I want everything, yet nothing at all.

Savior

I was walking through the valley,
With darkness closing in,
My soul was slowly dying,
And I knew that it would end,
Death was in my ear,
And sweat was in my palms,
I closed my eyes and ran,
As the wailing of pain wore on,
My body gave a shiver,
And my limbs began to tremble,
But then I saw a sparkle,
Smaller than a thimble,
I marched doggedly forward,
Until my feet left trails of blood,
And determined, I pressed on,
Until my breath was almost gone,
Slowly the thimble grew and grew,
And illuminated my frame,
A sweet and melodic voice rang out,
Happy that I'd finally came,
Tears drenched my face and cheeks,
And my God cheered with glee,
Because everyone had watched my struggle,
Everyone but me,
I looked back at the darkened path,
Happy to be done,
I got down on my knees and cried,

For God had watched me come,
And although in the dark I hadn't noticed,
He was with me all along,
For even in your darkest times,
He fights until they're gone.

Selah.

Thank you for reading Breaking Point
Love,
Chalay Hedge

www.ingramcontent.com/pod-product-compliance
Lightning Source LLC
Chambersburg PA
CBHW061303040426
42444CB00010B/2499